TWENTY-FIVE BENEFITS OF PULPIT EXCHANGE AMONG CLERGYMEN

BY

ARCHBISHOP OCHEI INNOCENT

Copyright reserved. No part of this book may be copied or reproduced without the prior written permission of the author.

Contents

TWENTY-FIVE BENEFITS OF PULPIT EXCHANGE AMONG CLERGYMEN 1

BY 1

BISHOP OCHEI INNOCENT 1

BENEFIT NUMBER ONE 4

BENEFIT NUMBER TWO 5

BENEFIT NUMBER THREE 7

BENEFIT NUMBER FOUR 8

BENEFIT NUMBER FIVE 9

BENEFIT NUMBER SIX 11

BENEFIT NUMBER SEVEN 12

BENEFIT NUMBER EIGHT 13

BENEFIT NUMBER NINE 15

BENEFIT NUMBER TEN 17

BENEFIT NUMBER ELEVEN 19

BENEFIT NUMBER TWELVE 21

BENEFIT NUMBER THIRTEEN 23

BENEFIT NUMBER FOURTEEN 25

BENEFIT NUMBER FIFTEEN........29
BENEFIT NUMBER SIXTEEN........30
BENEFIT NUMBER SEVENTEEN..32
BENEFIT NUMBER EIGHTEEN 34
BENEFIT NUMBER NINETEEN 36
BENEFIT NUMBER TWENTY........38
BENEFIT NUMBER TWENTY-ONE
....40
BENEFIT NUMBER TWENTY-TWO
....42
BENEFIT NUMBER TWENTY-THREE...43
BENEFIT NUMBER TWENTY-FOUR
....44
BENEFIT TWENTY-FIVE................45

DEDICATION

To those who want to make the best of their ministry.

"Do your best to present yourself to God as one approved, a worker who does not need to be ashamed and who correctly handles the word of truth."

- 2 Timothy 2:15

FOR THE AVOIDANCE OF DOUBT

By pulpit exchange we refer to the mutually agreed decision to invite other guest ministers to your ministry.

And they too invite you in return.

It should not be by legislation or by compulsion by mutual understanding of the benefits.

Do you know all the benefits?

BENEFIT NUMBER ONE

Pulpit exchange enables you to bless people of other congregations outside your place of calling. Jesus Christ said to his disciples: let us go over to the other side for this reason also have I come.

No minister is called specifically for one congregation. This can be seen from the great commission which tells us to go into the nations teach and disciple them.

Therefore you cannot start and remaining with one congregation all your life and ministry.
You must from time to time go over to the other side. Therefore, you must not be a local champion.

BENEFIT NUMBER TWO

Pulpit exchange helps the hosting congregation to break monotony. Human beings generally take delight in diversity. That includes diversity in what they hear or listen to.

God gives men choice over several things. In the things which we have choice and even where we live. Nature abhors Monotony.

Inviting another guest minister to your puppet it's like a breath of fresh air to the people.
When a person alone ministers to a congregation week in week out it becomes monotonous. Sooner or later the person's message becomes highly predictable.

One good way to break this is to invite guest ministers or in another language exchange pulpit with other trustworthy ministers.

One minister alone cannot have all the gifts that there are in ministry. A minster should therefore look for somebody who has the gift that he or she (pastor) does not have and invite such a gifted person to his ministry.
Remember that when you fail to invite guest ministers that have the gifts that you do not have, your members will find a way to sneak out and attend other ministries in search of such gifts.

BENEFIT NUMBER THREE

Pulpit exchange creates opportunity for other ministers under you to exercise their own gifts.

When can you receive an invitation and you travel to minister other probably younger ministers will have the opportunity of taking care of your own property while you are away.

On the other hand if you refuse to exchange pulpit or honor the invitation of another minister you fail to allow the younger ones under you the opportunity to minister.

How then do you want them to gain the much needed practical experience?

BENEFIT NUMBER FOUR

Exchanging pulpit with your fellow minister is a sign of trust for one another.

When a person invites you to minister on his altar know that the person trusts you because nobody will give his pulpit more than once to a traitor.

The person is inviting you to partner with him in building the church and not to destroy it.

The first time is a mistake but the second time can only be folly or foolishness.

BENEFIT NUMBER FIVE

Pulpit exchange if nothing else adds value to your ministry. There are some persons that when they step into your ministry what good things that had not been happening before begins to happen. These persons do not only carry fire they also carry value!

It is also a known fact that only those who can edify your congregation qualify to take your microphone.

Close your eyes for a moment and imagine what will happen if you are in a young minister and such world famous ministers as Papa Adebayo or the late Kenneth Higgins when he was alive visits your ministry even for 30 minutes only!

That is why at Bishop Emmanuel *Mekomou* says even if your motor has knocked engine, look for somebody whose motor is moving and your own will also reach where both of you are going!

BENEFIT NUMBER SIX

We exchange pulpits to build new relationships for ministers of the gospel.

It enables the person inviting you guys to know you better by hosting you over sometime even in his own home.

This enables him to have a close contact with you and to access you and know whether you are worthy of association.

Since you are likely to behave well, this leads to stronger ties between you and your host and in the end builds stronger ties among ministers for the sake of the gospel.

BENEFIT NUMBER SEVEN

It can further open doors for new or more ministers. First of all there will be pulpit exchange and if after the exchange trust is built, both ministers having developed trust for one another and seeing the other minister as trustworthy will find it easy to recommend one another to new set of friends and associates.

The opposite of it is that when you have the privilege of ministry on another person's altar and you mess up, you can never be invited again and can never be in a position to recommend somebody else.

Your conduct has closed the door for many other ministers that could have come after you just as a good behavior can always open new doors to other people.

BENEFIT NUMBER EIGHT

It prevents ministerial burnout by giving the minister a refreshing experience. Most times, the host congregation goes extra mile to make a visiting minister comfortable.

Contrary to the above, it is a known fact that one's home congregation often takes him or her for granted. Those of us who pastor congregations will bear witness to the fact that no matter how long you preach and how much you shout on the pulpit your home congregation will just be looking at you! They might not think of even giving you a bottle of Coke to refresh yourself.

However the same you appearing in a new environment will be treated like a king!

Little wonder that people say you don't go where you are tolerated but where you are celebrated.

The local congregation hardly knows how to celebrate her Shepherd and that can be very frustrating.

The good news is that going out on exchange of pulpit from time to time can renew your mind and make the difference.

Some local church environment can also be very starchy. Leaving there for some other place once in a while refreshes you.

BENEFIT NUMBER NINE

It makes it very easy for ministers of the Gospel to reach other nations. One open door leads to another by the Grace of God.

You and I know that going is very necessary for us: The great commission tells us that we should go into the nations, teach and disciple people of the mission field.

We know that your local congregation can sponsor you to anywhere in the world. This can be done now or later in the future.

Imagine however the relief it will be when you know that another ministry in another nation, for instance or another city, is hosting you at their own expense!

That relieves even the home congregation because such money can be used to finance other projects.

Another good thing about it is that you can also meet there with more people who will take you to other nations and cities! Indeed before you know it you have gone right round the whole world with your ministry at little or no cost to yourself or your home Ministry!

BENEFIT NUMBER TEN

Exchanging pulpit with others enables your congregation to hear things that are hard to say. These are things that if you the pastor should say it, the home congregation will think that you are saying it because you need money or because you love what they can give.

Believe me I'm speaking from experience: there are some basic biblical truths that when you tell it to your congregation in person, they think that you are just talking because you will be a beneficiary. You know that man has a dirty mind.

An example is giving generally or paying tithes in particular. Unfortunately many members of the local congregation wrongly believe that the pastor is only trying to feather his own nest whenever the resident pastor is talking about paying tithes!

Our experience has shown that a way out of this challenge is to invite a well-respected guest minister who can come and teach these hard things.

We all know that you also know what to teach as a resident pastor but the truth is that because your congregation has known you so much and for so long, they take you for granted and feel that you are saying what you are saying just because it will benefit you.

A guest minister will be in a position to say some hard truths to the congregation, I dare repeat. Most times it is a confirmation of what you have already said and which they needed to hear from another person.

BENEFIT NUMBER ELEVEN

Number 10 point above reminds me that in the multiple of counsel there is safety. Out of the mouth of many witnesses the truth is established.

When one or two guest ministers come around and teach the same thing even the doubting Thomas's in the congregation tend to accept it as the basic truth of life.

Carefully chosen guest ministers help to reinforce the biblical truth that you are teaching.

Permit me to digress: The above is why it is always good to know the doctrine of the guests before he or she is invited so that he or she will not use the given 45 minute-sermon to scatter what you have used so many years to put together.

Needless to say that you must shine your eyes well before you pick a guest minister to exchange pulpit with.

That however, does not mean you will be so afraid that you never invite others. The benefits of inviting others far outweigh the other.

Remember also that fear is not of God. Fear is of the devil and most times is aimed at stopping you from doing the needful.

Rather than submit to fear, each time you invite a guest minister watch carefully. Do not hand the person your microphone and go away. Be there to watch and be sure he or she can be trusted and if he or she makes mistakes, correct him or her in their presence but in a polite way.

BENEFIT NUMBER TWELVE

It helps to raise funds.

Mainly due to the fact that the congregation is used to a particular man of God who incidentally is their regular pastor find it to respond to his call for funds. However when another minister comes visiting and makes the same request, the same congregants rush out with great enthusiasm.

The story has been told in another book of a man of God who another minister once invited to minister. Within the twinkle of an eye the guest minister was able to raise a humongous sum of money.

The host minister was so shocked that he began to ask aloud before everyone whether it was still the old congregation he had pastured for years or another one

They say in my village that a prophet has no value in his hometown. We have said something similar before.

Therefore and more importantly, permit me to say that some people have the gift of fundraising. They have either the training or natural flair for doing so.

You can exchange pulpit with such gifted persons to take advantage of that gift in meeting the fundraising goals of your ministry or chapel.

May I warn that such invitation to others to raise funds should be once in a while! Let it be at that particular time when there is a need for the funds that you hope to raise. Since this book is targeting mainly the clergy it will not be my responsibility to tell you when and when not to raise funds.

I suffice it to remind you that the Bible says do all things in moderation. That applies to even when you are inviting guests to raise funds.

BENEFIT NUMBER THIRTEEN

That brings us to the issue of discipleship.

A minister that is into pulpit exchange with others will be conscious of the need for somebody to take care of the home church when he or she is not around. He or she must raise disciples that can take his place when he travels out.

When there is no one to take your place or no one to do exactly what you can do, when you travel out, then who will take your place when absent?

Necessities force us to train people as Bible instructs us to do in Ephesians 4 and ensure that they are capable of keeping the place going while we arc away.

Without that, church work or ministry will suffer greatly in our absence.

Exchange of pulpit, opens our eyes to the above need especially when the exercise is regular.

BENEFIT NUMBER FOURTEEN

The exchange of pulpit leads to greater church growth. This is so because to enable you keep going out you need to manage the ministry or church professionally just as a manager does with a company.

Every church grows numerically, financially, environmentally and spiritually.

Because you need to travel, you make plans and set goals ahead of time. You also organize the people and other resources to meet your set goals and timelines.

Part of it but not all, is the issue of discipleship earlier discussed. When we train and raise other people we are on track because it is people that are the church. The more your disciples grow in knowledge, the more the church grows in evangelism and other things that bring people to church.

Not only that: the more you travel out, you also get to see how others decorate their environment and that inspires you to go home and decorate your own church.

So the church grows environmentally and numerically.

It also engenders other forms of growth such as financial growth: Most times people return from their outreach ministry with extra funds with which they finance deficits at home. It is mainly the big Ministries that are able to finance everything about their outreach on their own while young and growing ministries get funds from the mission field or their outreaches!

Such funds may not be regular and predictable. The fact remains that with prayers all things are possible.

I remember a trip we made to Burkina Faso and I was short of funds. We had some failures in transportation arrangements prepaid. Before the problem could become a disaster God sent a man whom I knew from nowhere to give to me enough money to cover our return without begging.

Such things are known to happen on outreach ministries and talking about outreaches has to do with exchange of pulpit.

When things are working financially, environmentally and spiritually, they are bound to rub off on the numerical growth.

While a church or ministry needs to be led spiritually, effective management sees to it that there is numerical growth. We must not forget that the Bible says wisdom is a defense and management is a manifestation of wisdom.

BENEFIT NUMBER FIFTEEN

Having a pulpit exchange program could introduce your ministry to new dimensions of prayer. Ws2wawsssvsvvvgswvgdeggegegf2111 Years back I used to think that we were praying a lot in our ministry but when I visited some other Ministries as a guest speaker and saw the level of prayer going on in those Ministries I realized that we were playing.

Result of it was that I went home and gingered my people to increase the prayer backing for our Ministry. You know very well that inspiration can come from anywhere particularly in the house of God.

Mingling with the right people will open your eyes to your own deficiencies and if you have the mind of Christ in you will learn from them instead of you wallowing in jealousy them!

BENEFIT NUMBER SIXTEEN

Pulpit exchange partnerships open new homes for your family members to holiday and have a little break or asylum when the need arises.

I remember those early days when my children were in secondary school and I would need to travel sometimes together with my wife that meant that we could not possibly leave the children on their own at home. It was quite easy for us to send them to the homes of the pastors we had visited in the course of Ministry and found to be very conducive for their stay.

That is a major advantage of exchanging pulpit with people because you will get to know them better and also to know their homes and how they can be useful to you.

I have said the above without prejudice to those Ministers who prefer to put people in hotels and those who prefer to be put in hotels. For me I prefer to bond by staying in your house and look forward to you bonding with my family by staying in my home.

If we cannot protect our individual privacy and confidences then something is wrong with our Christianity. But that is my personal opinion.

BENEFIT NUMBER SEVENTEEN

To avail the Church of Christ with specialized knowledge, some ministers of the gospel are endowed with specialized knowledge and skills that are relevant to the growth and development of the church.

Partnering with such persons and making your platforms available for them to be a blessing to your people is a plus to the kingdom of God.

Apart from being a journalist, I am one who later took some trainings in management, ending up as a chartered management consultant.

Some of my friends have had occasions to invite me to minister things that could empower the youths of their

Ministries and they have not hesitated to tell me thereafter how so much my ministry has been a blessing.
One of them once asked me to talk to the youth who are suffering from acute joblessness in the country on: 100 businesses you can start with 100 naira only.

Some months later the pastor confirmed that some of the youths had actually become entrepreneurs supporting the church with their tithes!

A white pastor will watch out for those who have specialized knowledge in some areas to come and be a blessing to their ministries just as we earlier mention that those who have gifts that we don't have spiritual gifts should be invited to be a blessing or regular and exchanged pulpits with.

BENEFIT NUMBER EIGHTEEN

It promotes the sharing of information between ministers.

While hosting one another they take advantage of the meeting to share other useful information that will help the kingdom of God and the advancement of Christianity in particular.

Carefully arranged and supervised pulpit exchange is complementary and not competitive.

It is an arrangement that ensures that churches help one another and promote the unity that is required in Christianity worldwide. This help could be in the area of collaborations and joint programs with other ministries which are other forms of pulpit exchange.

It is a mutually beneficial arrangement that prospers the kingdom of God in all ramifications.

BENEFIT NUMBER NINETEEN

It promotes effective church management. Since the minister will be out of the church from time to time he has to be both tactical and strategic in his thinking and planning and in the setting of goals to be made and by whom. He has to plan in advance what each department has to do when he is there and when he is not there.

A well-planned ministry does not allow anything to happen unexpectedly to eat. Rather everything is forecasted and both set to upcoming events and those who are to handle what are contacted long before time.

A well-managed church comes up regularly with a roadmap of activities and timelines as well as financial goals and potential guest ministers are invited with enough time for them to prepare.

Viable work teams are created in such a way that their engine will keep working even when the principal or head of that ministry is absent for any reason such as a pulpit exchange.

BENEFIT NUMBER TWENTY

When there is an arrangement for pulpit exchange each time the guest speaker comes in, committees are set up for the reception and members of this committee get to learn the worth of ministers of the gospel in general as they prepare to host them.

Those who know what to do and reasons why such should be done, pass the information to those who do not.

Sooner than later, the whole church gets to learn the full worth of ministers of the Gospel and how best to host them and how best to host them: not so much about food but prayer friendly environment for instance.

This in turn rubs off on the host minister because members of the committee will now be wondering whether the guest speaker they just treated so very well has two heads or only one just like their resident Pastor! Chinua Achebe said in one of his books that when mother cow is chewing grass, the young one is watching the mouth.

As the resident pastor leads the people to comfortably host the guest minister he is indirectly teaching the congregation how best to treat a minister irrespective of whether he is hosted or the resident minister.

With the above repeated regularly in the church, you find that the hosting church will soon start doing the same thing for their pastor. After all, what a man sows, he reaps.

BENEFIT NUMBER TWENTY-ONE

Pulpit exchange provides you with a perfect opportunity to exhibit both your home training and ministerial ethics.

Many people tend to miss behave when they think that they have traveled very far away to places where no one knows them. What they fail to know is that bad news travel faster than light!

No matter how well you can pretend they say everyday carry one bucket to the well the time will come that this bucket hold have the bottom of. They say you can fool some of the people some of the time but never all the people all the time. One day perhaps in a moment of indiscretion the person will without planning to, exhibit his true colors.

That is why every minister of the gospel must endeavor to be fully trained and disciplined for that is the only way to sustain an exchange relationship.

BENEFIT NUMBER TWENTY-TWO

Pulpit exchange arrangement enables you to meet, mingle and minister with persons you might be meeting for the first time. Someone might connect you but it goes beyond the person who introduced you: You get to meet with total strangers.

Thus, it becomes an opportunity to show love to total strangers and not just people that you see every day and who probably know your house and have a chance of requiting your Love.

It gives you the chance to touch people in distant places. People that in your normal course of duty, you would not have reached at all.

BENEFIT NUMBER TWENTY-THREE

Sometimes your wife might have to travel with you. **This provides a very big opportunity for your wife to see other women in action and learn**. The activities of the other women she will be meeting in the mission field will be an inspiration to her. Most importantly the way the wife of the other minister receives people will be an eye-opener to your wife if she had not been up and doing.

Going on an exchange is a great opportunity to school because your wife will get to see so many things that other women are doing particularly how to receive people into her their home with a cheerful face and how not to be a bully to other women or one that destroy her husband's Ministries. These are things that will be easily land because she will see those things in action except where the other ministry has problems.

BENEFIT NUMBER TWENTY-FOUR

This arrangement also boosts our equipment, musicians, choir and all other workers.
I was once the guest speaker in Onitsha, down town Eastern Nigeria. Being there afforded me the opportunity of seeing their band at close quarters. I admired the equipment and if in Excel of both the magicians and the choir.

I went home to implement all the things I saw and heard which helped that other ministry to have a very vibrant, well choreographed and well decorated/equipped music department and musicians.

BENEFIT TWENTY-FIVE

It validates (or crucifies) your ministry before man. God knows your ministry and what it stands for but man believes what he knows about your ministry or what he thinks or what other people think about you and your ministry.

Unfortunately man walks by sight. Most times they judge you with whom they see you. If you move with a scandal prone pulpit exchange partner, chances are that you will be scandalized. If on the other hand you move with a well-known gentle man in ministry, one who's doctrines do not run counter to Christianity, they will accept you.

The Bible did not just say we should flee from sin alone. The Bible tells me that I should flee from all appearances of evil. in plain language we should avoid actions, places and conditions that do not portray us as Christians even though we are Christians at heart!

When we exchange pulpit with certain people it becomes a plus.

ABOUT THE AUTHOR

BISHOP OCHEI INNNOCENT IS THE PRESIDENT OF NEW DIMENSION SEMINARIES INTERNATIONAL.

HE IS A MEMBER OF THE INTERNATIONAL FELLOWSHIP OF THE CHRISTIAN CRISIS CENTERS, USA.

HE IS MARRIED TO LIZZY AND THEY ARE BLESSED WITH FOUR GOD FEARING CHILDREN.

THANKS ONCE MORE FOR READING THROUGH

newochei@gmail.com

I ENCOURAGE YOU TO REACH ME WITH SUGGESTIONS YOU HAVE FOR THE IMPROVEMENT OF THIS BOOK IN THE NEXT EDITION.YOU CAN ALSO LEAVE AN HONEST REVIEW ON AMAZON.

ONCE MORE I THANK YOU FOR CHOOSING TO READ THIS BOOK AND I PRAY THAT ONE WORD REMAINS IN YOU LIFE FROM THIS LITTLE BOOK. -BISHOP OCHEI INNOCENT.

OTHER BOOKS BY THE SAME AUTHOR

1. HOW TO DEAL RUTHLESSLY WITH THE SPIRIT OF CONSPIRACY.
2. HOW TO DEAL RUTHLESSLY WITH SIN.
3. HOW TO DEAL RUTHLESSLY WITH USE AND DUMP SPIRIT.
4. HOW TO DEAL RUTHLESSLY WITH HATRED AND RACISM.
5. SO YOU CALL YOURSELF A PASTOR?
6. SO YOU CALL YOURSELF A MANAGER?
7. SO YOU CALL YOURSELF A HUSBAND?
8. HOW TO COUNSEL A MAD MAN

9. WHY IS CHAPLAINCY NECESSARY?
10. HOW TO HANDLE REBUKE
11. HOW TO KNOW A MALCONTENT BEFORE YOU MARRY HER.
12. 2050
13. SOMETHING WORSE THAN WITCHCRAFT AND ACIDIC PRAYERS TO DESTROY IT.
14. WHY A GUEST SPEAKER MUST ASK QUESTIONS BEFORE MOUNTING THE PULPIT.
15. WHY MANY PROPHETS HAVE SMALL CONGREGATIONS.
16. THE REAL REASON: WHY MANY GIRLS ARE NOT MARRIED.
17. WHY THE WORLD IS AS WICKED AS IT IS.
18. DANGERS OF MINISTERIAL ARROGANCE.

19. INTRODUCTION TO TRANSPORTATION CHAPLAINCY
20. INTRODUCTION TO GOVERNMENT HOUSE CHAPLAINCY.
21. REJECTED
22. HOW TO QUICKLY DEVELOP DEPENDABLE PASTORS
23. WHY IT IS NOT ENOUGH TO PREACH ONLINE
24. OPEN YOUR MOUTH WIDE LIKE MILLIONAIRES AND LET THE WEALTH FLOW
25. HOW TO CHOOSE THE BEST BUSINESS TO DO -FROM HOME NOW: THINGS TO CONSIDER
26. BENEFITS OF BEING A CHRISTIAN
27. ESCAPE FROM A CHRISTIAN PRISON

28. SEVEN WAYS A CHRISTIAN CAN BE A WITCH WITHOUT KNOWING
29. DUTIES OF AN ARCHBISHOP
30.

NOTES

NOTES

www.ingramcontent.com/pod-product-compliance
Lightning Source LLC
LaVergne TN
LVHW052103160826
845678LV00015B/3329

* 9 7 9 8 7 4 6 7 0 2 2 5 8 *